Good Luck
along the Way

Robert Eugene Jenkins

Contents

Life Is About Choices Good or Bad

The following will be a history and other information of the life journey of Bob. I am seventy-seven years old, and I'm writing this from memory from September 10, 2013, and later.

Time Line

December 14, 1935—Birth—Alvarado, Texas

March 1951—Quit High School—Dalton, Nebraska

September 1952–March 1953—Nebraska National Guard—Dalton, Nebraska

March 1953–December 6, 1956—Joined the Navy—Sterling, Colorado

July 27, 1958—Married Wilma Joyce Endsley—Mt. Erie, Illinois

July 1960–August 1961—College—Eastern Illinois University—Charleston, Illinois

September 13, 1961—Birth of Son James Michael Jenkins—Charleston, Illinoi

September 1962–December 31, 1990—Worked at IRS—Herrin, Illinoi

September 1962–March 1967—Worked at IRS—518 North Mill St., Olney, Illinois

February 2, 1967–December 31, 1990—Worked at IRS—1207 Willow Drive

June 10, 1964—Birth of Son Jerry Brian Jenkins—Herrin, Illinois

May 18, 2012—Moved to 1605 White Pine Lane—Kingsport, Tennessee

1935

I was born on December 14, 1935, in a small, two-room home in Alvarado, Texas. We lived in this house for six months, and we moved. I don't know where, but this was one of the many moves in my life.

My dad's name is Sidney Colquitt Jenkins, born on October 19, 1911. His middle name was for the governor of Texas. My mother's maiden name was Mable Lee Manning, born on August 31, 1916. My dad was six feet, three inches tall (more on this later), and my mom was four feet, eleven inches tall, so I ended up being five feet, nine inches tall.

Dad was red-headed with green eyes. People called him the red-headed Irishman, I don't know if we came from Ireland, but some of my relatives believed we did. Dad always wore a cowboy hat and boots, and he was very big at 190 pounds but not fat. I was told Dad worked at the King Ranch, the largest ranch in Texas, busting horses to ride when he was sixteen to seventeen. So when he went into a room, his head would touch the top of the doorway. He also looked like "John Wayne", more on this later.

I had a sister, Helen Virginia Jenkins born in Aubrey, Texas, on October 26, 1934, and died on October 27, 1934. Mom had several miscarriages and never had more children except for me who was born on December 14, 1935. Dad and mom tried to adopt a red-headed boy, more on this later.

Dad had two brothers and five sisters, maybe I will do a family tree. Mom had three brothers and five sisters. I married Wilma Endsley on July 27, 1958, and have two sons: James Michael Jenkins born on September 13, 1961, in Charleston, Illinois, and Jerry Brian Jenkins born on June 10, 1964, in Herrin, Illinois. I also have four grandsons: Tyler James Jenkins and Eric Hites Jenkins (Jim's boys) Jared Robert Jenkins and Corey Mathew Jenkins (Jerry's boys). I also have two daughters-in-law, Della Hites Jenkins and Rebecca Baker Jenkins.

Since my dad had red hair, my hair was somewhat red, and I was called *little red*. I had several fights with someone teasing me. My mother *always* called me Robert.

1941–1943, Age 6–7

The earliest time I remember was when I was five or six years old. This was the start of World War II (1940 or 1941). We were living in Oklahoma City, Oklahoma. I remember keeping our window shades down and turning our lights off after 9:00 p.m., and we had milk and ice delivered to our apartment, I don't remember ever owning a house.

We lived in Oklahoma City on the Twenty-Ninth Street. One time, a friend and I made a box kite and we flew it over the Twenty-Ninth Street, and the kite was stuck in tree on the other side with the string across the busy street. My father had only one lung and the military would not take him, so he worked in an ammo plant.

1943–1945, Age 7–10

We moved to McAlester, Oklahoma some time before the end of World War II in 1945. I do remember Mother buying items with tokens instead of cash.

My dad ran over a large rock and broke the transmission on his car. I did not have a bed in this place, so I sleep between two chairs butted together, and this was a one-room house.

Sometime when I was five or seven years old, we had a car accident during a time before seatbelts. I was standing in the front seat, I hit the windshield with my head, and had glass stuck to my forehead. I still have the scar.

Coffee! I was told my Dad would pour his coffee into a saucer, dip bread or biscuit in the coffee, and feed it to me. So I have had coffee all my life. My folks kept a pot of coffee on the stove 24-7. My dad smoked cigarettes, and for a time, my mother dipped snuff or tobacco.

1946–1947, Age 11–13

We moved to Pampa, Texas, the panhandle of Texas, after the war in 1945. I was seven or eight years old. Dad started to work in the oil patch as a roughneck. I went to a one-room school in the country, and I rode a horse to school sometimes. That was fun!

I had a paper route after we moved to town, and on the second day, a large St. Bernard dog jumped on me. I was scared, but all he wanted was to play and lick. I played with this dog every day. I used money from my paper route to buy a bicycle. It was a Schwinn Challenger bicycle with a horn on the front and I was so proud of it.

I folded the papers in an octagon shape to throw better. One of our neighbors had a pack of three greyhound dogs and an old car with the back seat out. We would put the dogs in the back seat and chase coyotes. The dogs could outrun the coyote and have it corralled. The man would shoot the coyote and take its hide to sell.

We moved three or four times. I checked into one school at 9:00 a.m., and on the same day at 2:00 p.m., we moved to another location. My folks looked into me going to an Assembly of God Christian school full-time at Waxahachie, Texas, at age twelve, which I did not do. I would have to live until my eighteenth birthday.

1948–1949, Age 13

We moved to Borger, Texas, when I was in the eighth grade. Borger was an old cowboy town. It had dirt streets with wooden sidewalks with tie-ups for the horses. The cowboys would have their spurs and six shooters. The town now has two colleges and lots of factories.

I remember one or two of my buddies placed a DETOUR road sign on the road pointing down a narrow, one-lane road. Cars and trucks filled up the road and could not get out. It took a long time to get the cars and trucks out.

I got a job working at a resale shop. The owner had me to set up a fireworks stand in the edge of the town. On the last night of July Fourth at about 10:00 p.m., I decided to buy a firework that goes along the ground. When I lit the fuse, the firework went straight to the stand and started a fire and *all* the fireworks exploded and could be seen for miles. My folks were coming to get me and saw the display. Also, the fire went up the light pole, burned out the transformer and the tavern up, and the streetlights went out. I worked the rest of the summer for free to pay off my debt.

This is when my life gets interesting.

1949–1950, Age 13–14

We moved to Stinnett, Texas, a few miles north of Borger, Texas, when I started my freshman year in high school. Dad was hired as a foreman in the oil patch and worked for a company called Huber Oil Company. This was the time the unions were trying to unionize the oil fields. The oil companies did not want the unions, and when my Dad was working for the union, he was fired from his job. We had a company house, which was in a camp of other oil field workers. This was one of the best houses we lived in at this time.

My folks moved to Sterling, Colorado, before Christmas. I did not want to move, so my folks let me stay with friends and finish the school year. This was the only school where I spent a whole school year, more on this later.

The summer before school started, a friend was given an old pickup truck. This truck had no cab and no fenders. We put new breaks and fixed a wooden seat and wooden bed for the truck.

This town had no trash pickup. My friend and I would pick up trash barrels for $1 each and drive two to three miles on a state road to the dump. Near the end of summer, we were stopped by a state trooper, and he told us to get the junk heap off the road. He did not give us a ticket. So this finished our business venture.

I turned fourteen, and in the state of Texas, I could get my driver's license. I started the school year making mostly Cs; however, I finished making mostly As. I liked school! This was a new school, and I was asked to help in the library. I became interested in reading, and I gave the most book reports than anyone in school. I read all of Grace Livingston Hill's books and all her daughter's.

I tried out for basketball, but since I was small and a freshman, I did not get to play much. I then tried out for the football team.

Since I was small, they made me a tailback. On about the third game, I was given the ball to run around the end. When I made the line, the biggest boy hit me so hard, I flew back five to six yards and had a concussion. I went to the coach's office the next day and quit football. Then I tried out for baseball, which I liked and was pretty good at. I played second base. On the second or third game, a boy who had filed his cleats to a razors edge slid into second and tore my left shoe. I almost ripped my little toe real bad. This ended my baseball career.

June 1951–September 1951, Age 15

When school was out in June 1951, I moved to Sterling, Colorado. I was fifteen years old. I got a job for a farmer in the summer of 1951. He took me out to a field and told me to plow the 40 acres. I did, but I went around and around. The farmer brought me lunch, and he laughed since he wanted the plowing to go diagonal.

That summer, the farmer had two grain combines and three trucks. We took them south to the top of Texas and combined wheat. I drove the truck. When we had to stop in Kansas because of hailstorms, some of the workers left. I started driving the combines. I was paid $15 per day to drive the truck and $20 per day to drive the combines. We finished in September 1951 in South Dakota. I started my sophomore year. Texas schools were ahead of the Colorado schools, and I took some junior-level courses. We moved to Nebraska before the end of 1951.

November 1951–March 1953

I moved to Sidney, Nebraska, with my folks. I started *high school* in the tenth grade. My folks were moving again to Wyoming in November 1951, and I refused going with them, and I quit school. I was tired of moving, so I left home at the age of sixteen. *Bad Choice!*

I got job driving a dump truck for the county. This lasted for two or three months. Then I got a job driving a semitruck, also known as an eighteen-wheeler truck, for a couple of months. Then I got a job at a twenty-four-hour truck stop. I remember one night, an eighteen-wheeler truck came to the station and had nails in every tire. It took me all night to have all eighteen tires took off the truck and repaired.

One night, four of us boys hit a buffalo. I was not driving, and no one got hurt bad.

This was the time I joined a local gang. We had a fight with another gang, and I used a chain as my weapon. The gang used three-teardrop tattoo on the left hand between the thumb and forefinger. I did not stay with this gang. I was told after our fight (I left around 10:00 p.m.) that at about 3:00 or 4:00 a.m., some girl was killed. I never saw it in the paper.

Nebraska Army National Guard

In September 1952, I joined the Nebraska Army National Guard. I lied about my age saying I was eighteen years old, however, I turned seventeen on December 14, 1952.

Sidney, Nebraska, gets lots of snow in the winter. One day, the unit was called out and took to an open field. We were told to get our shovels and picks and to unbury a trailer court under the snow. Later we were called out to rescue people trapped in a train in the hills where snow had blocked the train.

The National Guard unit was about to be sent to Korea. I was dating a navy recruiter's daughter, and he said, "Let me get you in the Navy."

I think he was trying to get me from his daughter. So in March 1953, I joined the Navy, my folks had to sign for me, and was sent to San Diego.

Good choice! I was put on a Destroyer USS *Fechteler* DDR-870 and sent to Korea for the war.

Bits and Pieces

Dad was a blue-collar worker, so we never made it to the middle class. He made better than average wages. We were not poor, but we lived from one paycheck to another. He worked in the oil patch. This meant he was a "roughneck". He worked on the oil-drilling units as a laborer and operator. He also drove big trucks that would carry the oil well drilling units from one location to another.

The roughnecks were a rowdy bunch—gambling, drinking, and staying in bars. Dad did very little of this until later on. Dad was a kind and gentle man even though he was a big guy. He was teased a lot because of his size and red hair.

Since Mom's father and stepmother lived in Cleburne, Texas, we had to drive to see them once or twice a year. Mom's dad, my grandfather Henry Reed Manning, worked on farms in the area, and in later life was a janitor at the local Baptist church. He was born in Texas on October 16, 1870. I was told my great-grandfather was a Baptist minister. His wife was Nannie Bell Williams. She was born in Mississippi on November 6, 1876. When she died, my grandfather married a lady by the name of Margaret. Nannie Bell died before I was born, so the only grandmother I knew was Margaret.

My mom and I would go to church, but Dad rarely attended church. He never stopped mom from going. Mom joined the Assembly of God church in the early '50s. One time, Mom and I went to hear Oral Roberts in Borger, Texas. This was a healing tent meeting, and what I saw turned me against religion for a long time. They had people walking up to the tent, getting into wheelchairs, and took in to be healed so they could walk. I was twelve or thirteen. One of mom's biggest disappointment was she wanted me to be a preacher. When I was eleven or twelve, I took violin and steel guitar lessons for a short time. Since we moved so much, I gave up on music.

We would visit one of my uncles, Herbert Jenkins (Dad's brother) in Oklahoma City. I remember the red dirt and an oil well in the backyard (not my uncle's). He worked at Tinker Air Force Base and was already retired at the time. He had one son named Bert Jenkins who worked for the telephone company in Oklahoma City.

We had only one vacation that I remember. We went somewhere in south or west Texas. We had a Jeep and camped in parks and alongside the road. I saw Dad get into the swimming pool at a park, and the water was so cold you could not stand to get in the water.

March 3, 1954–December 6, 1956, Age 17–21

I'm in the Navy now. This is one of the best things that happened to me at this time. I know the Lord was looking over me and with my mother's prayers. In Denver, I met a group of boys from Colorado. When we got off the bus from Sterling, Colorado, we were told to pick up papers and cigarette butts off the sidewalks.

We were put on a plane to San Diego, California to the naval base for boot camp. We were given a group of tests for our knowledge. Some of the boys told me to do real bad on the tests. The rumor was if you did real well on the tests, they would put you on some bad duty. I did my very best and received a good set of test scores.

On the second day, they took us to a swimming pool and told us to swim back and forth using the regular swim method, the backstroke, and the breaststroke. Since I could not swim, I cheated by having my feet on the bottom of the pool. I passed the swim test.

The next day, I was told that if I did not know how to swim, they would give me lessons. I told my company commander, and he said I passed, and he would not let me take lessons. To this day, I cannot swim very well. This is something in the Navy and not able to swim.

I was given a red stripe since I did not have a better education. This meant I would work on the ship's engines and be where it was hot and dirty.

On the third week, I walked past the main office and saw a sign asking for a radar position. I did not know what this was but knew it would be better than working on the engines. I went into the office and asked if the position was still available and was told yes if my test scores were high enough.

They checked my scores. I did qualify, and I got the job of a radarman. They gave me a white stripe. I took off the red stripe and put on the white strip. The next morning, I lined up with a white stripe, and my officer told me to take off the white stripe and go back to the red stripes. I explained that his boss gave me the white stripe. This was a *good* move thanks to God and my mother's prayers.

USS *Fechteler DDR-870*

I was assigned to the USS *Fechteler* DDR-870 in April 1953. After a shakedown period in the Long Beach, California area, we departed to Korea on May 10, 1953. One day before we left the Long Beach area, I saw the large seaplane practicing landing and takeoff. The seaplane was a Howard Hughes plane, also known as *Spruce Goose.*

This plane had eight engines and was the largest seaplane ever made. The office of the radar was just below the ship's bridge where the captain and others running the ship were located. Our duty was to keep track of all the other ships, planes, and submarines. We could see them on the radar screens, talk to the other ships, etc. We would always know what was going on and where we were going.

One time, I worked behind a large plain plexiglass where I had to track planes and had to write backward so the captain and others could read the board.

I was put on the destroyer, USS *Fechteler* DDR-870. We were part of four destroyers, and our ship was a radar picket. It had more radar gear than the other three ships. We left San Diego, California for Korea.

We went to Korea on May 10, 1953, and we left Korea on September 1, 1954. The war was over on October 15, 1953. We operated above the 38th parallel to keep other ships from bringing supplies to North Korea. We would capture the ships or blow them out of the water. Other times, we would stay behind an aircraft carrier to pick up any pilot who had to ditch his plane in the water. I did see some of this action.

There were over two hundred ships in this area. They would supply our ship by having a supply ship come along the side and send items over by ropes and cables. We had to put one boy over to the other ship because he was sick so he could be sent to a hospital. This was quite a sight to see.

One night, we were called out for general quarters or battle stations because it appeared there were two hundred planes coming our way.

The radar showed all these blips. The aircraft carriers put up all their planes and all the ships got battle-ready. One of the pilots called and asked how we wanted our geese cooked. It was a whole flock of geese in the air stream flying at two hundred miles per hour.

Postmaster

I was given another duty besides being a radarman, and that was to take over post office. I had to open the post office once a day to pick up mail, sell stamps, and process money orders and packages. Also, when we would get to a port, I had to take our mail and pick up our ship's mail and have it sorted to give to the guys on the ship. I always had lots of help to go get the mail. Also because of this duty, I did not have to do a lot of other duties. I had free passes always when we got to a port.

I started to take thirty correspondence courses to work toward my GED. I did complete this, and because of this, I was able to get my high school diploma (more on this later). I even took a junior college test and passed, but I never used it.

We stopped at Oahu, Hawaii, on the way to Korea. I spent some time in Waikiki Beach and in the bars. I could see Diamond Head from our ship. I did see the pink Royal Hawaiian Hotel. It was still there when Wilma and I visited Hawaii in October 2008.

Our first stop was Yokosuka, Japan. Nightlife was neat. I went to Tokyo to pick up stamps and other things for the ship's post office. Another sailor and I had a Jeep with a driver to take us to Tokyo. The driver almost ran over people. I had my .45 pistol, more on this later.

We next went to Kobe, Japan, for nine days of rest and relaxing. I was asked to have dinner at one of the natives' home. I don't know what I had to eat, whether dog, beef, or chicken. I did see some Japan's Buddhas. The nightlife was neat.

On our way to Subic Bay, Philippines, we passed the islands of Bataan and Corregidor. We left the Philippines and headed to the North Sea (above the 38th). As we were leaving the Philippines, a submarine tagged us and we could not find out if it was one of ours, so the four destroyers sank it.

We finally left the Korea area and stopped at Sasebo, Japan. We were to go home on the opposite direction. Our first stop was Hong Kong. One night, I was called out to be a shore patrol to help get a native who had stolen a small ship and was going down the bay. We caught the guy and found that he had paid some sailor money for the ship. We had to shoot over his head to get him to stop.

Then another night, the shore patrol was called out to stop a fight at a local theater. When we got to the theater, I was the last shore patrol going through the door. Someone hit me and sent me down some stairs; I got up and went back in the theater. The morning we arrived in Hong Kong, the building looked nice, white, and clean, but the front facing the ships had been white-washed. The back or side of the buildings had not been painted. Funny.

On the morning of September 10, the Jolly Roger flag was run up the mast after crossing the equator, and Neptune and his court came on board. At first you are a pollywog. You are changed into a shell back by having your head shaven, your backside sore, and you reeked of fuel oil. So now I am a shellback.

We next made it to Singapore. We then went to Colombo, Ceylon at the tip of India. We saw sitting and reclining Buddha, also cobra charmers and elephants.

I bought a really good diamond ring as Ceylon was noted for its diamonds. I gave this ring to a girl I had been writing to for almost a year. I never got it back. That's Okay. More on this later.

We made our way up the Red Sea to Aden and through to the Suez Canal. This was quite a sight. The two counties separated by a narrow ditch. Camel drives on both side of the ditch. Then on to Naples, Italy through the Mediterranean. We visited Pompeii and Naples.

On October 2, Admiral Flechteler, his wife, and his daughter visited the ship. Next, we went to Rome where we saw the Coliseum, Rotunda at St. Peters, the Victor Emmanuel Monument, and St. Peters square. One of the tours attended an audience with the pope at Castel Gandolfo.

Now we come to one of the most beautiful places in the world, Cannes, France and the Riviera at Nice. The USS *America* was in port and invited us sailors over for a party with a group of American college girls. The girls on the beach wore no tops.

We then made it to Lisbon, Portugal for a short stay. Then, we stopped in the Azores, an island between Portugal and the United States. We are on our way home, *but* we ran into bad weather caused by a typhoon. We had major damage to our ship. Most of the radar gear was tore off the mast; we had a hole in our bow and some ship supplies got flooded. The five-inch guns were twisted, our inside passageway was bent, and one of our propellers was damaged. The other three ships had some damage. We could not get out of the storm and had to follow it till we were near Greenland or Iceland. We had to have a sea-going tugboat come and tow us to Newport, Rhode Island, USA. The crew of the ship encountered seasickness and sleepless nights, and had sandwiches for breakfast, lunch, and dinner.

One night, we heard two merchant ships asking for help. We could not stop and help, and one of the two ships shank that night. We finally made it to shore at Newport on October 27, 1954.

October 27, 1954–November 1, 1954

Newport, Rhode Island

I was scheduled to go to electronic training (ET) school in Norfolk, Virginia on November 1, 1954. I was called into the captain's office on October 30 and was told I was being transferred to another ship. I told the captain I was scheduled for ET school. He said sorry but because of my rank (RD3) I was needed on the other ship. This school would have no doubt changed my life. Me and a few of my buddies took a bus to New York City. We spent a weekend and saw some of the city buildings and nightlife. I have a cruise book about that part of the Navy journey.

November 1, 1954–June 19, 1955

USS *Isherwood* DD-520

The USS *Isherwood* DD-520 was in the same port as the USS *Fechteler* DDR-870. On my way to USS *Isherwood,* one of my seabags fell overboard and I lost my camera with all my pictures. I had bought an Argus 3 camera in San Diego at the ship's store and had taken lots of pictures on my trip to Korea and all around through the Suez Canal. There were thirty ships being transferred to the west coast through the Panama Canal. This was the dirtiest place I had seen in all the other places.

We left Rhode Island on January 4, 1955 to San Diego. We stayed for two days and left for the far west. I was going back to places I had been before. After stopping off at Oahu, Hawaii, we went to Midway Island. This island was noted for their "Gooney Birds." These birds were big and had a six-foot wingspan. They were so large they could not start flying and had to run apiece flapping their wings. They could not stop running, so if anything or anyone were in the way, they would run into it or you. The same when they were landing. They would fly all day and fish. Planes could not take off or land when the birds were taking off or landing. We would chase the Gooney Birds.

Our next stop was at Yokosuka, Japan. We were a part of Task Force 77, a fast carrier attack force, and were called to defend and remove people from the Islands of Tachen. The Chinese was shooting and dropping bombs on the island. We went next to the Chinese border and shot our five-inch guns on their beach. The evacuation was successful, and we moved on to Subic Bay, Philippines. There, we put our ship in dry dock and cleaned and painted the ship. We then went to Manila, Philippines.

We went to Buckner Bay, Okinawa for supplies. The USS *Princeton* CVS-37 met us and we had two submarines to practice in a mock battle. As quoted from my ship's cruise book,

> Although there were nine other ships in the "screen," the subs seemed to have it in for the Ish and tried to come through or should I say under us every time. Never once did they make it, however, and our alert crew receives a "well done" from the Admiral.

However, one of the captains on one sub took a photo through the periscope and he had us in the crosshairs, which was taken after the mission. I have a copy of this photo hanging in my office.

Now we were off to Sasebo, Japan, where we went into dry dock to have our screws repaired. We stayed here for some time. We were off for Formosa Patrol. It appeared we might have more operations in the Tachen Island, but instead, we docked at Kaohsiung, China for a few days. We did get to see some Chinese girls in their split skirts. Our next stop was Hong Kong (this was my second trip).

We next went to Kobe and Hiroshima, Japan. Hiroshima, Japan, was where one of the *A* bombs was dropped on Japan during World War II. Then we left for Yokosuka, Japan. On June 3, 1955, the cruise was over. We again stopped at Midway Island on to Pearl Harbor on June 11, 1955. We arrived in San Diego, California on June 19, 1955. I do have cruise book for this trip.

I have no memory about the next trips of the USS *Isherwood* DD-520 except when we were in Long Beach, California for a short time. Then we made another trip to the far west. I know we stopped on an island named Guam. I do know we stopped on Latitude 00'00 and Longitude 105'21'E to have our initiation to be a shellback. This was on June 11, 1956. I was already a shellback. However, the rules are: The shellbacks hide the Jolly Roger flag, and if the pollywogs find the flag before we have the initiation, then they get to initiate us. The pollywogs did find the Jolly Roger, and the captain let the pollywogs initiate us shellbacks. Then the pollywogs decided to let us initiate them so they could get their shellback badge. I remember one of the boys that I knew hit me real hard when I went through the beltline. Then when we got our chance to initiate them, I paid the boy back real hard, and later, we became friends. On this trip, we were going to go to Australia, but a typhoon was in our way, so we went to New Zealand and New Brunswick instead. Then we came back to San Francisco, California. We did pass a small island named Jenkins. The captain said, "This was my island." I have no cruise book on this trip.

The sunrise and sunsets were beautiful and good to see. I saw lots of whales and dolphins and flying fish. One of the ships ran over a whale and I am sure it killed the whale.

I was discharged from the Navy on December 6, 1956. I was on San Francisco, California naval base. I enjoyed the Navy and almost stayed in the service, but I knew it would not be a good thing to be married and have children. I would have received the rank of Petty Officer Second Class on my way to becoming a Petty Officer First Class.

January 1957, Age 21

Now Starting Another Life

My folks were living in Fairfield, Illinois, when I was discharged from the Navy on December 6, 1956. I stopped in Warrensburg, Missouri. I stayed at a girl's house with her parents. I don't remember her name. I had been writing her for some time. We were not engaged. I did buy her a set of China when I was in Japan. She found out I could apply for a small college in Warrensburg and start in January 1957. A buddy in the Navy had gotten us together to start writing one another. She was very nice, but since I had not seen my folks for over two years, I elected to go to Illinois and wait for college later. It was a mutual understanding for us to stop writing one another. I never saw her again.

My dad's brother, Uncle Terry Glen (TG) Jenkins had gone to Fairfield, Illinois, in the 1930s and started his own oil drilling business. In 1940, he had owned a three-hundred-acre land in Texas near their hometown of Cleburne, Texas. Then he also started a cattle feed lot in Kansas City, Kansas. He also owned a ranch in Wyoming, which covered a forty- to fifty-mile square. I know this is a lot of land. My Uncle TG hired my dad to be a roughneck to look after his oil wells in Fairfield, Illinois. This was in late 1954. My uncle owned one of the largest houses in downtown Fairfield, and he had the only Black maid. He had my grandfather Henry Jenkins come live with him from somewhere in Southern Texas. When Dad and Mom moved to Fairfield, my uncle had my grandfather to live with them. He was hard of hearing. It was told he had fallen off a bridge he was working on and broke his hearing in both ears. I moved in with my folks.

In November 1956, my uncle had three thousand heads of white-faced cattle shipped from Texas to Fairfield, Illinois. The people of the area said that was quite a sight since they had to drive the cattle some five miles to a farm my uncle owned along Highway 15. He had a cowboy from his ranch in Wyoming to feed the cattle.

My uncle hired me to help the cowboy, I don't remember his name. My uncle also bought three hundred areas of farmland in Massillon County and had my dad and mom move on the farm to plant corn to be used for the cattle. My dad did plant corn and harvested it for the cows. My uncle wanted to use the cattle markets in St. Louis, Missouri, Louisville, Kentucky, Evansville, Indiana, and other local markets.

When we finished feeding the cows for 180 days, he sold the cows to a market in Evansville, Indiana for twenty-one cents per pound on the hoof for the cows. The morning before the trucks arrived, the cowboy and I had all the cows up near the loading docks. The trucks came to the loading area early one morning and could not see anyone, and one trucker blew his air horn. Then all the cows ran all over the place. It took us a week to gather most of the cows, and the trucks came back. In the meantime, the livestock market dropped to ten cents for pound. The Evansville, Indiana market went broke on this one transaction.

My uncle had the market pay him before they picked up the cows. I had bought a new 1957 Chevrolet with a stick shift and a six-cylinder engine in green and white color. I used some DX oil, and it locked up my motor. The company with DX replaced the car, but this time, I got a 1957 Chevrolet with an eight-cylinder engine, hardtop red over white, automatic drive with racing cam and tires. I did go to Louisville, Kentucky, twice to drag race. I did not win anything, so I quit.

History

There were several gangs operating in southern Illinois during the 1930s, 1940s, and early 1950s. One gang, the Sheldons, lived in and near Fairfield, Illinois. Another gang lived in and about Herrin, Illinois.

These two gangs had a fight in Fairfield and Herrin. They had some bombs dropped on each other from airplanes. The downtown Herrin has some buildings with bullet holes in the outside walls. In the '40s, there was a movement to unionize the coal miners in southern Illinois. Near Fairfield, Illinois, some ten or twelve miners were killed.

The State of Illinois hired Charley Harris who was part of the Sheldon gang to stop these two gangs. He was to be paid by farmland south of Fairfield, Illinois. He killed several gang members. He was a bad guy who feared no one. He was not a good neighbor. He killed his wife and her lover by shooting and burning them in a house on his farm, and he was never convicted. However, he did kill one of his neighbors and was convicted and died in prison.

Restart

My uncle had drilled some oil wells on the land owned by Charley Harris. He asked me to drive one of his new pickups to check on some of these wells. When I crossed into Charley Harris' land, he shot at my pickup, hitting the driver's side and putting some holes in the door. I did not stay long and turned around in a hurry and went back to town and told my uncle. I asked him if he wanted me to go the police. He said, "No, just go get the door fixed and be sure it has his name on the door."

I did go back to Charlie's place to check on the oil wells. He did not shoot at me again. Once, I went with Dad to work on one of my uncles' oil wells. I let one of the pipes slip out of my hands and it hit Dad in the head. Fortunately, he had a steel hat. This did not hurt Dad but put a dent in the hat. This is when Dad decided I was not big or strong enough to work in the oil field.

We went to a tavern after this incident to get a beer. While we were sitting at the bar, some guy came up to Dad and said, "I understand the bigger they are, the harder they fall." Dad told him he had heard that the smaller the guy the further they go, and he picked up this guy and knocked him out the door. He never came back to the bar. Dad has always been picked on because of his size. He never wanted me to work in the oil field as a roughneck.

I started looking for a job when the cattle-feeding was finished. I tried selling insurance for Prudential Insurance Company for two weeks. The guy who was training me told me to oversell life insurance to people who could not afford. This was so he would get two to three months' commission, and when the people dropped the insurance, he would go back and resell the policies again and again.

I did not want to oversell these people, so I did not want to sell insurance. Then I looked into buying a gasoline truck and selling fuel to farmers, but found it was too expensive. Then a man in town told me I could work selling illegal beer or liquor in the dry county of Wayne. He would pay for any fines I would get from selling the illegal beer or liquor. I did not like this, so I did not continue this job.

I got a job with an oil field supply store. They sold parts and other supplies for the oil wells. I also fixed down hole pumps for the wells. The name of the store was Eagle Supply Company. Mr. Chet Mcquire was the owner. He had three stores: one in Flora, Illinois, one in Carmi, Illinois, and one in Fairfield, Illinois. I worked in all three stores. In late summer, I was working at the Carmi store. It was a very hot day, and the store was a tin building with no air conditioning. This day, one of our customers came into the store after lunch and found me lying on the floor. I had passed out. I was taken to the local hospital. I had lost too much salt, so I was to take salt tablets.

In the summer of 1957, five girls from the local neighborhood rode horses down past the farmhouse where I was staying with my folks. They were checking out the new guy on the block. I had my eye on one of the girls and thought I would ask her for a date. That never happened; instead, I asked one of the other girls for a date. She said yes. Her name was Wilma Endsley. *Great choice!* This turned out to be best date in my life.

Wilma was a senior in high school. We dated the rest of the year 1957, and in March 1958, I proposed marriage, and she said yes. I asked Wilma's dad Virgil Endsley for Wilma in marriage. Then the next weekend on a Sunday, her folks and my folks had dinner at Wilma's house. I told everyone about our engagement. This was not the best move. I know this embarrassed her mother Bertha. On one of our dates we went on a hayride, and I was holding Wilma's hand. I thought I was holding her hand, but instead I was holding another girl's hand, and when I looked at this girl, she was smiling.

My folks left Fairfield, Illinois, and went out west Wyoming (I think!) to work in the oil field. I stayed in Fairfield, Illinois. Neither came to our wedding.

Wilma and I were married on July 28, 1958, and we moved to an apartment in Fairfield, Illinois. I still had my job at Eagle Supply Company and Wilma got a job with an attorney, Harold Harrison. I was making $200 a month and Wilma was making $25 a week with $19.88 take home. This $19.88 was enough to buy food. We were happy newlyweds.

In the fall, one of the boys I worked with at Eagle Supply Company said he wanted to go to college. He was a high school grad with good grades. I said to him, "Let us ask our wives if we could go to college."

The next morning, he came in to the store and was sad since his wife said no for him going to college. I was all smiles since Wilma had said, "When and where are we going?" *Good choice!*

1958–1962

College

Fairfield High School would take my GED and give me a diploma, but I had to pass a Constitution test. I did pass this test. I thought about going to the big school University of Illinois, but decided it was too big and applied to Eastern Illinois College.

I had to sell my 1957 Chevy because I could not afford the payments and go to school. I did have the GI Bill benefits to help pay our bills since I was a veteran. We would get $225 a month. We sold our car for some guy to take over the payments and lost what we had paid on the car. We bought an old 1949 Chevy Coupe and had to make lots of repairs, which did not last. We then traded for a 1956 Hudson. It was a car that was no longer being made, but this car only had a few miles and looked like it was new. We had this car all the way through college even if we had to replace the head gasket and head several times.

We bought a twenty-eight-foot, old camping trailer and moved to the Charleston, Illinois. We parked our trailer one block off campus in the backyard of a person named Replogle.

Eastern was mainly a teachers' college. However, the fall I started college, it became a university. It was decided I needed to attend a summer session on English. I had decided to go into Accounting instead of Engineering since I did not have the best math background. It was discovered the accounting textbook was the same author I had in my correspondence course. Since Eastern went to the university system, I received a BS degree instead of a BA degree. The cost was very small, and we could also rent our textbooks.

I don't know how I made it through, but I did with the help of Wilma and some of the teachers being nice to veterans. I started in September 1959 and finished in the summer of 1962. I met a friend and a veteran, Buddy Addis, and his wife, and we have been friends ever since. He was in Accounting, and we studied and had several classes together. He had finished high school and had better grades (although I did have a B average overall). He passed the CPA exam, and I did not. I decided not to continue for this.

I worked at the student union for one semester, and then I got a job as a bookkeeper for a local grain elevator. I got this job through a local CPA office. Wilma got a job with a local attorney, Murvin Beal. He did not have a very big business and he would be gone a lot of times, so Wilma had to be at the office alone a lot. One time, Wilma did not get paid, and I went to Mr. Beal's house and asked for her money.

After this, Wilma found another attorney, Mr. Jack Anderson, who was a better choice, and he did become a local judge. Wilma always got her paychecks on time. She had a lot more work.

On September 13, 1961, our oldest son, *James Michael* Jenkins, was born. We moved to a three-room apartment on the other side of town in Charleston, Illinois. Our apartment was one block from the downtown square where Wilma was working. There was no married housing available at this time. However, a married housing apartment at the college did become available. One of my collegemates and I moved our stuff along with baby beds and a deep freeze we had won at a local store. When we had most of everything moved, it was found the married housing apartment was too small and we moved all our stuff back to the old apartment. When Wilma came to the old apartment and saw all the stuff still in the place, she wanted to know what happened. I told her not to ask since I had moved twice that day.

___

Job After College

I graduated at the end of summer in August 1962. I applied for several jobs, one with a local manufacturing company in Mattoon, Illinois. I did have an interview, but I did not take this job. It was for a Quality Control position. I wanted an accounting job. I applied to State Farm Insurance, but did not hear from them until after I had taken a job. I went on a job interview with the Ohio Oil Company in Finley, Ohio. I rode with another student to the interview. They gave us a test, and I did better than my friend. He got the job because he had been a student of the interviewer.

The Tax Man Cometh

The Internal Revenue Service (IRS) came to the campus and I decided to interview just to have additional experience. They invited me for another interview in Springfield, Illinois. They offered me a job as an IRS Agent at Herrin, Illinois. I was not familiar with Illinois and I asked where is this place. They had a large state map on the wall, and they showed me where Herrin was located.

I said I would take the job since I did not have any other job offers. I was married and had one son and would need a job. This was a *good choice*. This had to be a God thing since I found out that I was the only one hired at this time. The IRS had hired three or four guys in May.

Herrin, Illinois, was about sixty miles from my wife's Wilma's home area. I thought I would stay with this job for two or three years, and then find a job in the Accounting field. Once I had five years with the IRS, I decided to stay and retire with thirty years' service since I could use my military time as part of the thirty years.

I told myself I would treat people or taxpayers like I would like to be treated, and I did.

August 9, 1962–March 1967

Herrin, Illinois

Our oldest son James Michael Jenkins was about one year old when we moved to Herrin. We did not attend church anywhere. One day, a man from the United Methodist Church visited us and I told him we would think about attending. He said, "Whenever you make up your mind, you will attend some church. I will not be back to bug you."

A neighbor's girl named Dodie came and told us our son James (Jim) just about fell into a well in our backyard. The other kids said this girl saved Jim.

The house we rented had an old coal-burning heat stove in the basement, and twice a day, we had to clean out the unburned coal and put them on our driveway.

Our second son Jerry Brian Jenkins was born in Herrin at the hospital on June 10, 1964. We moved to another rent house in Herrin to be in another school district. In March 1967, we moved to Olney, Illinois, which was closer to Wilma's home area. More on this story later.

August 9, 1962–December 31, 1999

Internal Revenue Service (IRS)

The IRS office was in the basement of the Post Office in Herrin, Illinois, with an outside door. The IRS did not have a school for me in Springfield, Illinois, since the boys hired in May was still attending. I had to go with other agents and watch. One morning, they said they had found a school in Los Angeles, California, asked if I would like to go, and I said yes. I had been there in the Navy.

The IRS sent me to Los Angeles, California for my three-months basic training since they had no classes in Springfield, Illinois, and I was the only person hired at this time. Then they sent me to Buffalo, New York for my advance training. They sent me west and east for school and sent me to the Midwest to work. Funny.

The three months seem to be a very long time from my family. Wilma and her younger brother Allen Ray Endsley drove to Los Angeles, California, to where I had an apartment. It took them three full days. Wilma was twenty-two years old and Allen Ray was eighteen. They left our one-year-old son with her mom and dad, Virgil and Bertha Endsley.

Wilma said that Ray was driving down the mountains and she was telling him to slow down. He said to her, "Do you want to drive?" She said no, and did not say another word. When they got to the California border, Wilma called and said she would see me soon. I told her it would take another four hours. I took them to Hollywood and other places. We went to a Mexican restaurant, which was Wilma's and Ray's first time. I told Wilma to taste the sauce and she took a big spoonful and found it was very, very hot. She now loves Mexican food.

In the IRS schools we would read the tax laws and have tests. When I finished these two schools, it was the same as having a master's degree in taxation.

Some IRS Stories

The tax law is simple: Code Section 61 says that *all* income is taxable unless there is an exemption or deduction. I always treated taxpayers like I would like to be treated.

Ninety percent of my audits were good and no problems. Most of the taxpayers were cooperative and had their records available. I had one taxpayer who owed a lot of money saw me on the street and said, "Hi! Come see me, but leave your brief case at my office."

There was a story where a taxpayer was being shown around heaven, and St. Peter said the old run-down houses are where the pope and ministers live, and the castle is where an IRS agent lives. When he asked how this could be, St. Peter said, "Well, the IRS agent scarred more people into heaven than the other people."

One of my first audits was a young, single lady. When she came into my office, she was crying. I asked why she was crying, and she said her buddies told her she was going to jail. I told her no, she was not going to jail. As a matter of fact, she was entitled to a refund. I thought if all my audits would be like this, I would not like it.

There was a mob gang who operated a tavern and girl house in Colp, Illinois, nine miles from Herrin. One of the agents in our office had one of the gang members, Junior Hatchet (his mother's name was Ma Hatchet), to come to our office. I was on the counter to answer taxpayers' questions when he came into the office. He had a bodyguard who was wearing a gun on this short-sleeved shirt. I told him he had to leave the gun at the main desk and not take it back to the agent's office. His boss Junior Hatchet looked at me, and then told the boy to give me the gun. I don't know what I would have done if Junior Hatchet had not given it to me. This gang finally moved to East St. Louis, Illinois, and still operates in the area.

I had a man come to my office with a box full of business receipts. He dumped the receipts on my desk and on the floor. He said there you are! I told him, "No, it is not." I told him that if he did not pick up these receipts, I would have the janitor to put them in the trash and have them burned. He said I could not do that, and I said you had better call your attorney or accountant. He did call his attorney and came back and said he would pick up all the receipts. I also told him that I was not going to sort through the receipts and that he had to do it in our library. He did!

I was a field revenue agent, and most of my work was at the taxpayer's home or the attorney or accountant's office.

I was told to call the taxpayers and schedule appointments. Once, I called and talked with a lady and told her I wanted to schedule an appointment. She fainted and fell to the floor. I called the local police, and they found the lady. She was all right. I told my boss that I would send a letter asking for appointment from now on. He was not very happy but never stopped me from sending letters.

I scheduled an appointment with a company in another town and was given directions to his shop outside of town. I went to this location and saw a car parked next to the shop and a motor running inside. I went to the door and knocked and since this was a business I went into the building. A huge dog hit me upon going into the building. I jump up on a tractor. No one was here, just me and the dog between the door and me. I picked up a large wrench and hit the dog and killed it and left. I called the taxpayer and he said, "Oh, I intended for you to come to my office downtown."

I told him I had killed his dog. He said he would have me fired and I told him I would have him arrested for trying to harm a federal agent. He did not have me fired. I believe he did this on purpose. More on this story later.

I had one audit, fraud case, that took thirteen years to complete. It was a large million-dollar case, and the taxpayer kept changing attorneys, and we had three criminal court trials. He was never convicted even though he was guilty. He had several other audits and finally died before serving any prison time.

One time I went to Springfield, Illinois, 130 miles from Olney, Illinois, for two weeks. Wilma did not know I actually went to New York City for an undercover assignment. Wilma would never know whom I was auditing. If she would need me, she would call the office and they would find me and tell me to call her.

Once I went on an audit with another agent, a special agent who carries guns. His name was Robert Eugene Jenkins, and when we told the taxpayer we both had the same name, they did not believe until we showed them our badges.

Another time, I went with a revenue officer, he did not carry guns. We were met at the front door by the taxpayer who had a shotgun. We left, went to town, and had a federal marshal bring him into our office.

I went to a farmer's house to ask if he had bought some cows from another taxpayer I was auditing. He said yes and told how much he had paid. As I was leaving, the farmer said he had a confession to make. He had only filed one tax return in forty to fifty years. I did an audit on six years and found he did owe some $40,000. He had saved this much over the years, and he wanted to pay the bill. He lived in the country and never had a car or truck. His family walked everywhere. They had three children who had all finished college and were teachers. When I left the last day, the taxpayer had a suitcase on the front porch, and I asked if he needed a ride into town. He said, "No, but aren't you going to take me to jail?"

I said no.

February 1967–May 20

Olney, Illinois

I made a decision when I was about to be released from the Navy. I told myself that what I wanted in life was a good wife and have a family and live a medium-income level. I was never looking to make a fortune. I knew with my educational background I would be limited in how far I could go in life.

When I was given the opportunity to move to Olney, Illinois, I said yes. *Good choice.* This was a town closer to Wilma's home area in Massillon township near Fairfield, Illinois, in January 1967. I went to Olney and found a small house on North Mill Street to rent and moved the family in February.

The little two-bedroom house had a floor furnace between the kitchen and living room. It was a gas furnace. We had to watch our boys James and Jerry from this furnace because it could get hot. This house was three blocks from the grade school, and James would walk to school even in the snow, rain, etc. This house was two blocks from the local hospital. We met some people who lived one block from our house who had two boys about our boy's ages and one older girl.

Our boys and our family became good friends with the Van Matres: Frank, Pat, David, Jeff, and another family member whose name I can't remember. James was in the first grade in the Silver Street School, and Jerry also attended this school when he was old enough. We looked at several churches in town and decided to attend St. Paul United Methodist. This was the smallest of three Methodist churches but had a group of kids and the people were friendly.

I wanted to get both boys involved in Boys Scouts (Cub Scouts). I went to the Presbyterian Church to enroll James, and I was told by the scoutmaster that he would not take my boys. I don't know if he did not like me or what? I called the main office in Evansville, Indiana, and was told they could force the issue. I said no, I would just start our own Cub Scout unit at St. Paul United Methodist church. We had it until both boys finished the Cub Scouts. They did not want to continue since they were going into basketball and football.

We bought our first home in March 1970 at 1207 Willow Drive, formerly 23 Willow Drive. It has three bedrooms, one bath, and double car garage. It was only three years old and in the nicest part of town. It was between the grade school, middle school, and high school. The boys walked to the schools most of the time or rode bicycles.

There were three city grade schools namely Cherry, Central, Silver Street, and a Catholic church school. These were all big rivals in basketball. Our sons James and Jerry went to the Silver Street school. Darnell Jones went to Central school. The brothers Tony and Tim Jennings went to the Catholic school. More on this later.

When our boys were still in grade school and middle school, we met some friends namely Richard and Levona Hard. They had a fold-down camper and said we should get one and go camping with them. I saw a camper for sale on the next block, so we bought our first fold-down camper after we moved to Willow Drive. We went camping several times with the Hards. It was contest of who could setup their camper first. We generally lost since they had three children and we had two. It was fun trying.

We bought another newer fold-down camper since the first one was so hard to set up. Wilma's younger brother, Ray Endsley (Ray bones) bought a fold-down camper, and we went to Washington DC in 1976, and then we went to Yellowstone the following year. The Hards moved to Oklahoma City, Oklahoma. One summer we were to meet them at the Lake of the Ozark in Missouri, about halfway for both of us. On our way, we had a flat tire on the camper. We fixed it and went on our way. Then one of the tires came off the camper, I think it was the one I had replaced, and the camper's top came off and threw our stuff on the roadway and tore up the camper. We got a U-Haul trailer and got what we could and left it in a junkyard.

We went on to the campsite and stayed with the Hards in their camper. We then bought a tent and used it a few times. It was a tall tent where you could stand up and we had some backpacker's type sleeping pads. It was not too bad, but we did not like it when it rained. More stories about camping later.

Family–Fabulous Wife and Great Kids

The next several years seemed to fly by so quickly, and so much happened that I might not get everything told in the correct order.

In the fall of 1969, I took a part-time job teaching accounting, taxes, and small business management at the local two-year college, Olney Central College. I taught for nine years. This gave us extra funds for when our boys were in college. The IRS also had me teaching tax schools throughout the state of Illinois. I had to prepare my own chapters to teach. The schools were called Farm Income Tax Course. It started out for farmers only but later was for CPAs and tax practitioners. I also did my own tax seminars.

Wilma worked for Presbyterian Church as a secretary for five years, and then for Bakerline Oil Tools for five years, and then for Doctor Herbert Brokhof DDS for five or six years.

James (Jim)

He was always on the go. He was always good in school. He started in the fifth grade playing basketball, and since he was generally taller than the other boys, he got to play a lot.

The town of Olney, Illinois, had three grade schools and a Catholic grade school. There was always competition in basketball. Jim has friends in each of the schools. Jim and some of his friends made it to the varsity basketball team in high school. They had good teams. They won conference, sectional, and super sectional their junior year. This is the last game to be play before the state title. Their winning number was twenty-six wins and five losses.

Their senior year, they won the conference but lost in the sectional. The story is: the town of Effingham went to Germany over the summer and brought back a seven-foot boy. Jim's school was given the option to go to Germany, but they could not raise enough money to send the whole team. This seven-foot boy started in college in one of the best schools in the area, did not stay, was drafted into the professional basketball teams, and finally gave up basketball. I don't know what happened to him.

Jim was playing in a tournament at Benton, Illinois, and he had a very good game. He scored thirty points with fifteen being free throws. He was working on some thirty free throws as a record. A college basketball scout was at this game and talked with us about coming to his school for a tryout. He did and was given a two-year scholarship at Three Rivers Junior College in Poplar Bluff, Missouri. This school had one of the best win records of any other junior college in the US.

The coach Mr. Bess had a book written about him with the coach with most wins in junior colleges with three thousand wins. He had a team at the national tournaments most of the time. They had won the national tournaments the year before Jim got there. They went to the national tournament both years and won third place. The second year, they had a record of thirty-three wins and no losses. Jim had straight As and even helped one of the other players. They lost a last-second shot which would have put them in the finals. This was very disappointing.

Jim went to University of Illinois for the next two years and received his Accounting degree. He had very good grades.

Jerry

He was never as tall as Jim. He was short like me. He took after the Manning family. However, he was always a competitor in anything he wanted to do. He did play basketball through his freshman year. He broke his arm playing touch football in PE.

He did play football the last two years of high school. He was a running back. He scored the winning touchdown against the rival team at Mt. Carmel. Olney had only beaten this school very few times.

Jerry always had good grades and did not seem to have to study as hard a Jim. In the seventh and eighth year, the school set up a middle school with no inside walls. This was concept from California. They would let the students have one hour a day to go the library or sit in on other classes. Jerry would sit in on other classes and this is when he got interest in chemistry. He later went to University of Missouri at Rolla, Missouri and received a chemistry degree. He received the second highest in his class. When he started junior year, he had to declare his major. When he was in line for his classes, he intended to go for petroleum. However, the boy behind him wanted the petroleum engineering, and there was only one more slot available. Jerry decided to go for chemistry degree. This turned out to be a *good choice*. More on this later.

Dad and Mom Moved to Olney, Illinois

In 1973, my dad and mom moved to Olney, Illinois. I knew for a long time that my dad was an alcoholic, and because of this, he was having problems keeping jobs. He never drank much at home. He was always going off to work in other places. Because of this, I talked Dad into applying for disability through Social Security. This would give him money to help Mom in making a small living.

I even got Mom and Dad an apartment for low-income housing in a small town ten miles from Olney and also had Dad a part-time job doing odd jobs for the housing project. I did not know how bad Dad's alcoholism had gotten. The house Dad and Mom rented in Olney, Illinois was three blocks from my office. Before Dad and Mom moved to the apartment, Dad called and wanted to talk to me. I walked the three blocks to their house. I noticed there was a suitcase on their bed and Dad's boots on the floor. I thought he was going to leave again. We just talked about general things, and he told me he wanted me to take care of Mom.

Mom was working for a nursing home. Later that day at about 5:00 or 6:00 p.m., we heard an ambulance (we lived close to the hospital). Wilma and I received a telephone call from the police station that my Dad had shot himself in the backyard of the house they rented. I think Dad thought he was doing us a favor since he was sure he could not give up the alcohol. We moved Mom to a low-income housing project in Olney.

Raymond Shann

Five or six year later, Mom meets and marries a man by the name of Raymond Shann. He had a farm eight miles West of Olney with a nice three-bedroom house and a basement. He had no children, and his wife died several years prior to Mom meeting him. He had a travel trailer and a pickup. They went to Southern Texas for the winter. Raymond lived for about three years. Mom inherited the house, travel trailer, and barns. The will gave the land to great-nephews. Raymond had asked me if I wanted the farmland, and I told him he needed to leave it to his family. We traded the trailer for a small, twenty-four-feet motor home.

It was easy to drive, and we took it to several camps for Mom. After some time, Mom was having heart problems and we had to take her to Vincennes, Indiana to the hospital. One late night, Mom called and we made a flying trip to Vincennes. It was decided to move Mom to town in Olney, IL so she would be closer to the hospital and doctors. Later, we moved her to a very nice assisted-living place. She lived there until she had to be moved to a nursing home where she later died at the age of ninety-two.

More Camping and Vacations

We became friends with several people who liked to camp. We did a lot of camping in the local campgrounds in the area for the weekends. Once, we were in a Square Dance Camping club and we would go to different towns that had square dancing and camp for the weekend. This was a lot of fun. Usually, we would square dance on Saturdays in our town once a month and other towns the other time. We had our own square dance caller who would give us lessons.

First Retirement

On December 14, 1990, I would be eligible for retirement with more than thirty years of service (twenty-eight years with the IRS and four years Navy) at age fifty-five. Before December 1990, I had forty-quarter Social Security coverage, but after December 31, 1990, I would not have forty-quarter coverage since the law was changed. I knew I would need to work somewhere to get the necessary coverage.

Attorney Frank Weber from the Weber, Tedford, and Heap Attorney Firm called and wanted me to train his two boys on income taxes. I worked in the Robinson and Newton offices for two years. I started my one tax practice. I also worked for two other accountants for two years. The tax practice keeps growing until we had some six hundred clients. With Wilma's help, we did several bookkeeping accounts.

Another Adventure

We were given the opportunity to work as a tailgater for a camping company in 1990. Our neighbor two houses from our house had worked for this company for many years. He had gone to Alaska several times. They were going to Alaska in couple of years. We thought this would be fun and we went on two trips. A tailgater was a camper who was the last trailer and had to stay behind the other campers to help if needed. We paid for the first trip to see if we would like it or not. We went around Lake Superior into Canada. There was an older couple in the '90s that had an old motor home. They were always the last to leave the campground and would stop to rest along the way. When they got to the next campsite, they did not care if their camper was level or not.

The next trip in the summer of 1991 was in Washington, DC, and the Outer Banks in South Carolina through Pennsylvania and Williamsburg, Virginia. We stopped off on the way back in Kingsport, Tennessee, to see our son Jerry. This time, we were paid and given free camping. It was a very interesting trip.

We were looking forward to the next summer when we were to go to Alaska. However, during the winter, we were told the camping company was sold to another company and that they did not want Mr. Bates or us to be employed for the new company. We thought about finding another camping company, but did not pursue this idea. Then this is when we started our tax business.

Second Retirement

My mother passed away in August of 2008. Wilma's mother passed away on June 20, 2009, one day after she turned ninety-seven. At her funeral, I fell down the concrete basement steps at the West Church near Mt. Erie, Illinois. I banged my head on the concrete wall and landed on my right shoulder. Della and Tyler took me to Vincennes, Indiana, to the hospital, while Wilma, Jim, and Eric stayed at the church for the funeral.

I suffered a concussion and messed up my rotator cuff where I had already had surgery a few years before. I had several weeks of therapy and decided to close my accounting and tax business. So we decided to go to Florida for the winter months. Friends Frank and Pat VanMatre told us about a place to rent. After Christmas, we went to Avon Park Florida and rented a place, then we ended up buying a similar place in the Villa Del Sol Senior Park where several other Olney couples stayed during the winter. We saw an orthopedic surgeon in Orlando, Florida, and he advised me to get a shoulder replacement, but that I should return home and see a specialist in St. Louis, Missouri. So I saw Dr. Keener at Barnes in St. Louis and had a reverse shoulder replacement on May 11, 2010.

May 18, 2012

Moved to Kingsport, Tennessee

In the summer of 2011, our son Jim said we should move to be closer to him or to Jerry, our other son. Jim and his wife Della and family lived in St. Louis, Missouri. Jerry and his wife Becky and family lived in Kingsport, Tennessee.

In September 2011, we went to Jerry's place and stayed with the boys while they went to California a few days for their anniversary. We looked at some places to buy. We saw some nice places and condominiums for people over fifty-five. Later in September, we went to St. Louis where Della had a realtor show us some places. We put a retainer on a place but on the way back to Olney, Jim called us on the cell phone and said he had found there were more fees we did not know about.

We decided the additional fees was too much and told Jim to cancel our offer on the condominium in St. Louis. We called the realtor in Kingsport and said we wanted to make an offer on one of the condominiums, so we bought a place there just before Thanksgiving of 2011. We had this new place painted inside while we were in Florida. We went to Florida in December and did not move to Tennessee until May 18, 2012. In the meantime, we were trying to sell our house in Olney, Illinois. It did not sell before we moved to Kingsport. We were there only about a month when it sold.

Of course, right off the bat, we went to a couple different Methodist churches. Jerry said we should get involved with First

Broadstreet on Church Circle because they would have a lot of things for seniors there. We joined and really enjoyed the fellowship there. We have a very active Sunday School class, and we also attend the church's Wednesday nighters which always have a nice meal for $7 each and a program. It has helped us meet a lot of nice people.

We scheduled appointments with new doctors. After we were there a few months, I noticed when I walked in the neighborhood that I felt pressure in my chest. It is not flat anywhere in Tennessee, so I told the new doctor about it on my first visit. He scheduled some tests and learned there were some problems.

We took a trip to Illinois for Wilma's family reunion and had an appointment scheduled for a heart catheterization after we returned. There were too many blockages for stints, so I had a triple bypass surgery on September 10, 2012, by Dr. Myers, who was originally from Chicago at Holston Medical Center.

Jim came the day before the surgery. He stayed for three days until I was doing better. I think he approved of the doctors and medical care I was receiving.

I have gotten involved with a Korean War Veterans Group here and attend monthly meetings, and we visit at the Veteran's Hospital in Johnson City, Tennessee. I really enjoy this group of men. I also joined a genealogy club at the Senior Center. We meet monthly and these ladies have taken me under their wing. They have been doing genealogy for many years and have tried to teach me a lot.

Grandchildren

Jim (James) and his wife Della had two boys named Tyler James and Eric Hites. Jerry and his wife Becky had two boys named Jared Robert and Corey Matthew.

Tyler James Jenkins

Tyler was like his dad—always on the go. He was always tall at six feet, six inches, and he played basketball, like his dad. He played on teams in the summer, and sometimes his dad was the coach. He played basketball and football all four years of high school.

It was odd his football coach had him playing offensive center and not a wide receiver. He was always very strong. His football team was always very good. They played for the state championship on Tyler's second year. Tyler did not try out for a basketball or football scholarship since he wanted to go to medical school. He did go to the University of Missouri in Columbia, Missouri.

He finished his four years and two years medical school and is now in his third year of residency at Northwestern University's McGaw Medical Center in Chicago, Illinois.

He said, "I'm treating a gunshot wound." She said, "I don't care, you have to go next door. The patient next door was having constipation."

So much for a first-year residence, yes. He married Ashley Miles on May 28, 2011. She is also a medical student and going into dermatology. She is in residency at University of Chicago Medical Center. They both are working very hard. I am very proud of both of them. I think Tyler loves what he is doing, orthopedic surgery. After completing all their medical trainings, they have relocated to

Columbia, Missouri. They have four children: Luke James born on May 1, 2017, Elizabeth Kathryn (Ellie Kate) born on March 28, 2019, John Bruce (Jack) born on January 26, 2021, and James David born May 8, 2024.

Eric Hites Jenkins

Eric Hites was hearing impaired at birth. This was discovered when he was six months old. We had taken Tyler to Walt Disney World in Florida. While we were there, Jim and Della called us and said they don't think Eric can hear. They took him to their doctor, and he said no, he is bright-eyed and all. He is not deaf.

Jim's family lived in Springfield, Illinois. They finally had his hearing tested and Eric did have a hearing disability. They found a good school in St. Louis Missouri for hearing-impaired children of all ages. Della drove him to St. Louis to St. Joseph School for Deaf many days a week from Springfield. Jim found a job in St. Louis, Missouri, and moved the family in order for Eric to attend the school in St. Louis.

This has been a good move since Jim found a good job and Della has her own interior decorating business. When Eric was six, he was given a cochlear implant in his left ear. This has been a very good thing for him. He was tall in high school and he played basketball. He was feet, five inches, and is now six feet, six inches, like his brother. He received a four-year college scholarship to pay basketball at Fontbonne University in St. Louis, Missouri.

He was not getting to play much in the third year with a new coach as the old coach died, so he gave up his last two years of basketball. He graduated in December 2014 with a degree in Special Education and is now going for a master's degree in Deaf Education. He is a very busy guy with both school and substitute teaching. After finishing his education, Eric took a job as a Special Education teacher. On July 6, 2019, Eric married Lauren Maureen Dowdy who is a speech therapist. They have two children: Leo Hites born on February 23, 2021, and Anna "Annie" Maureen born on May 4, 2023.

Jared Robert Jenkins

Jared was born October 29, 1995, in Kingsport, Tennessee. Jared got involved with the Boy Scouts and went all the way and received the Eagle Scout Award. He is a very sharp in computers. He graduated from the South Sullivan High School in Kingsport, TN. He was also in the Air Force Junior ROTC and he ended up with a Lieutenant Colonel rank. He was also part of the Honor Guard all four years at Sullivan South High School. I was honored to present Jared the Korean Veteran's Medal for 2013–2014 for the senior year at South High School. He started college at the University of Tennessee in the fall of 2014. He took part of the money he received for Christmas and built his own computer. I have to call on him for help when I run into computer problems. Jared is working for a computer technology company in Colonial Heights, Tennessee. He has bought a condominium in Kingsport.

Corey Matthew Jenkins

Corey was born in Buenos Aires, Argentina in October 1998. He has two passports. I understand he will need to declare his country when he reaches his eighteenth birthday. Wilma and I were so blessed to get to fly to Argentina when he was two months old to see our fourth grandson. What an experience that was for us.

He is also about to get his Eagle Scout Award. He is in the band in high school and plays percussion drums. His band went to the Outback Bowl on New Year's Day 2015 in Tampa, Florida. We feel honored to be going to that event, and all the family went there except for Tyler and Ashley.

Corey finished his education with a Bachelor's Degree from East Tennessee State University. He attended a course in Barcelona Spain on teaching English in a foreign country. In November of 2021, he went to South Korea to teach English and did not know any Korean since he had taken Japanese for a foreign language. He taught English there for two years and came back to Kingsport for Christmas 2023. He is planning to find employment in the US.

I have enjoyed all my grandsons very much. We got to take Tyler and Eric camping several times. I have a lot of good memories. I can't forget how Tyler and I worked on the Missouri Badges when camping at different Missouri State Parks and how they loved the campfire pies. Since moving to Kingsport, Tennessee, I am getting better acquainted with Jared and Corey. They were able to spend a little time with us camping at East Fork Campground in Olney. I have enjoyed watching Jared in ROTC and going to parades to see them marching. Corey really does a great job playing his drums. We have stayed with them quite a bit. I think it is called grandparent watching to make sure the ole folks don't get in trouble.

We now have five great-grandchildren with another on the way. What a blessing to have such a wonderful family.

Dash

There is a story about the *dash* in a person's life. When you are born, (e.g. 1935–20??), what you do in your life between the *dash* is your life. I turned eighty years old on December 14, 2015, and have not yet reached the end of my *dash.* So I don't know what is ahead. I have had a good and interesting life. All my family has made me proud.

One of my golden rule is to *always do your best and do no drugs.* I tell all my grandchildren this rule every time we depart one another.

Life Goes On

I went to the Best Western Hotel in Johnson City, Tennessee, on April 21, 2016, to start a *great* trip with the Honor Flight of North East Tennessee. This was a free trip to Washington, DC, for World War II, Korean, and Vietnam veterans. Travel, meals, hotel, and other items were provided at no cost. There were four World War II and eighteen Korean veterans, one medical doctor, two EMTs, one Navy corpsman, and one minister. There were also twenty-two guardians (one for each veteran) and our leader (a lady—she was our sergeant). We had a great time and visited all the Memorials in Washington, DC.

In February of 2023, I applied through the Korean Defense Veterans Association (KDVA) for the 2023 Revisit Korea program sponsored by the Korean Government. The Revisit Korea program is for all veterans from all nations that served in Korea either before or after the signing of the Armistice on July 27, 1953. I qualified as I entered the Navy in February 1953 and was discharged in December 1956 after serving on two different ships in the waters around Korea. In July 2023, I received notification that I was selected as one of fifty veterans for the 2023 Revisit Korea program scheduled for October 10–15. Each veteran takes a caregiver on the trip, and I chose my Grandson Jared Jenkins to accompany me.

It was quite an honor to make this trip. I also have another Grandson Corey who lives in Seoul, South Korea and teaches English. We left on October 8 from the Tri-Cities Airport to Atlanta, and then a sixteen-hour flight to Seoul, South Korea.

Grandson Corey has lived in Seoul for two years, so it was an honor to see him. Our agenda with the Revisit Program started on the tenth, and our first visit was to Camp Humphrey which is the largest military airport in South Korea. We also visited the Seoul National Cemetery where we laid wreaths and participated in an Incense Offering Ceremony.

Since I was one of the oldest veterans, I was honored to be in front and helped with the Incense Ceremony. We also visited Panmunjom (the demilitarized zone) and the Changdeokgung Palace. One evening, we were treated to a banquet dinner where my grandson and I were seated with two four-star generals and the American ambassador to South Korea. There was a spectacular performance by a Korean Dance group for entertainment. I was also honored with several medals and a special Korean War hat.

During my years in the Navy, I had never set foot on Korean soil as I was always on a ship, so what an honor for me to be able to visit the country that we had defended.

I have lived a good life. I am now eighty-eight years old and been married sixty-five years and enjoyed every bit of it.

About the Author

Robert Eugene Jenkins was born in 1935 in Alvarado, Texas. He attended various grade schools as his parents moved around following oil field jobs in Texas, Colorado, and Nebraska. He quit high school after finishing his freshman year when his parents moved and left him behind on his own. He worked various jobs until he joined the Navy in 1953. After serving as a radarman on two different ships in and around Korea, he was discharged in 1956 and went to Illinois where his parents were living. He worked in a supply store, and it was there that he met his future wife. After one year of marriage, he attended Eastern Illinois University in Charleston, Illinois, on the GI Bill. He and his wife have been married sixty-five years and have two sons, four grandsons, and six great-grandchildren.